Adapt
or Die

Adapt or Die

How to Survive in the New Era of Digital Marketing

Applying the Principles of
Digital Brand Engagement to
Capture Marketshare and
Grow Your Brand

By Tom Gallego

L7 CREATIVE | Publishing

DEDICATION

To all those marketers who want a progressive
strategy to hit unrealistic goals.

Table of Contents

ACKNOWLEDGMENTS

I want to thank my team at L7 Creative who helped inspire and create this book. I am grateful for their hard work, passion, and devotion to DBE practices.

" *It is not the strongest of brands that survives, nor the most intelligent. It is the ones that are most adaptable to change.*"
— Adapted from evolutionist Leon C. Meggison's renowned quote

Introduction

As a modern marketer you need
Digital Brand Engagement (DBE) to adapt
and survive in a quickly-evolving marketplace.

In July 2016, personal product titan Unilever bought Dollar Shave Club for $1 billion. Yes, that's the same Dollar Shave Club that launched the now-legendary campaign, "DollarShaveClub.com — Our Blades Are F***ing Great," complete with a dancing bear, and a machete-wielding CEO. It was a campy, unique positioning that shook the men's disposable razor category to its core and weakened industry leaders.

Dollar Shave Club offers their customers a fresh shave anytime with low-cost blades delivered regularly to their doors. Using technology and low-cost manufacturing, combined with a clever creative strategy, the company addressed clear pain points in the market: razors had become increasingly expensive and what was available on the market was inconvenient to buy in a store.

The idea was good, but it wasn't mind-blowing. Dollar Shave Club showed its real smarts not in the innovation itself, but in the way in which it connected the right idea to the right audience.

The startup company didn't go after the entire addressable market, it targeted Millennials who it knew had adopted online subscription models to simplify their lives. That kind of drilled-down targeting is important to note: The company nurtured its highly targeted customer base with **strategies that didn't just sell to those consumers, but also engaged them. And engage it did.** Within an hour of launching its "Our Blades" video online, Dollar Shave Club found itself in the inconvenient, but nevertheless enviable position of having its servers crash from a flood of traffic.

A few years, millions of razors shipped, and a billion dollars later, Unilever acquired a unique brand that nails it with the audience and, as a result, gobbled up market share - some of that share was in fact Unilever's.

"Buy back my market share," strategy happens frequently. Giant consumer brands experience the onslaught of their market by innovative startups that not only offer breakthrough products, but that also adapt to evolving technology and rapidly changing consumer behavior. The big guys are afraid of smaller competitors that can play the consumer engagement game better than they can. In fact, they're afraid enough to spend billions of dollars to acquire them.

Effective Digital Brand Engagement isn't a nice-to-have option that gets whatever is left in the marketing budget, after accounting, for all the usual channels. It should be a **vital foundation of your marketing plan to make the difference between success and failure at the enterprise level.**

Why have the effectiveness and value of so-called "traditional" channels fallen so quickly behind the new DBE way? In a word, **ENGAGEMENT.** In a complex, digitally linked world, one-way, push-my-message-out-and-see-what-happens strategies no longer work. **Connection matters more than communication now.**

Three factors, then, make DBE a must-have for every company today:

- Media channels are so fragmented, it's impossible to understand them all.
- Audiences have broken down into insanely narrow market segments.
- Marketing automation is a lie.

I. Media fragmentation and the paradox of choice

There was a time during the last marketing era when most senior marketing executives could conceivably put together a one-page list of all the media channels that fit their ad strategy. Within hours, the experts could draw up a budget to buy media on those channels. Provided they had creative in the can, they could then buy the media, have their message reach a critical share of their addressable market within a matter of days, and get results. **Not anymore.**

We've seen a stunningly fast decline in the effects of mass media in just the last 5 years — sort of like the dinosaurs at the end of the Mesozoic era. Today's DBE era affords so many more media options that it's exceptionally difficult to remain disciplined in all of them. Sociologist and author, Barry Schwartz coined an apt term for this particular phenomenon: "The Paradox of Choice." The more options we are presented with, the less effective our decision making becomes and the less satisfied we are with the choices we make. Conversely, "paralysis by analysis" can occur as a result of the new digital ecosystem.

Many marketers, challenged with constrained resources as well as the fast-moving nature of today's marketing space, either rely on a mix of traditional and digital channels or simply resort to the old "throw-stones-at-the-mastodon-and-see-if-we-can-bring-it-down" approach. Some rely heavily on the latest tactic, "du jour", which can result in brand confusion, and serious inefficiencies.

II. Hmmm, where did my audience go?

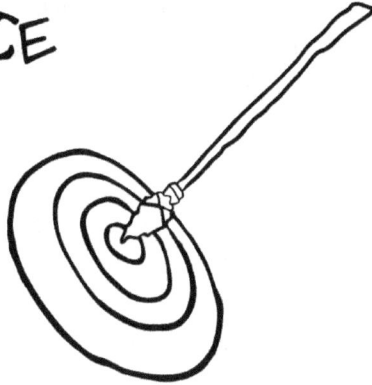

TARGET AUDIENCE

✓ FEMALE
✓ LIVES IN MANHATTAN
✓ WEARS FEDORAS
✓ CROCHETS

Figure 0.1 – A sub–niche, or even a sub–sub niche, can be created for just about any shared human interest, no matter how narrow.

R emember the adage "get rich in a niche?" It's alive and well as consumers buy more goods than ever before in increasingly slim segments where their particular interests lie. The fragmentation of media options is now exceeded only by the fragmentation of audiences. One side effect of the incredibly advanced targeting and segmentation tools offered by digital platforms is that every sub-sub-sub-niche you can imagine can be targeted by products specifically positioned for it.

Today you aren't just competing with a short list of top brands in your industry. Instead, you often go head-to-head with specialists targeting dozens of tiny niches within your space – and even individual freelancers or contract manufacturers that can sell directly to your customer from anywhere in the world.

Just as a broad media strategy will no longer cut it, a simple demographic representation of your audience is useless. Your micro target audience is most likely made up of dozens of cliques, each with its own attitudes, needs, and social media preferences. To properly reach all of them — without destroying the consistency of your brand — requires the tools and strategies found in this book.

III. So-called marketing-automation actually delivers neither

If you could swipe your credit card for a few dollars a month and "build long-term relationships with your customers" or "control your content, channels, and marketing performance," or any of a hundred other pitches to upgrade your marketing tactics, wouldn't you jump on that? Yep, you would.

No doubt you've heard these false promises, but don't be fooled, marketing automation is not your salvation.

Don't get me wrong, these tools can be an indispensable part of a DBE program. **But it's critical to understand what these products are — and what they aren't.**

Suppose you had the most technologically advanced automobile factory, complete with hundreds of robotic tools, but your vehicle lacked a design. Would you produce a best-selling car? Or any cars at all for that matter?

Make no mistake about it, marketing automation tools don't provide you with unique positioning, a defined niche audience, or a brand message that will resonate. In one sense, they do deliver automation (the routinely mechanized working of a machine, process, or system), but they don't do the one thing that matters most: create a marketing strategy for you. Marketing automation systems still require substantial effort by humans to input the strategy into their tool set. Fundamentally, they remain just tools to organize and manage the delivery of messages to people and measure the effectiveness of those messages.

Of course, software is better than people at things like keeping track of dozens of customer segments and targeting them with specific messages at set intervals. So as a marketer, you need marketing automation software. But no matter how much you might want it, no software exists that will relieve you of the need to devise a unique, creative, and effective marketing plan.

IV. It's not really that bad, is it?

By starting with a clearly defined DBE strategy and strong brand assets, you can create efficient and effective marketing programs. The consumer journey has undergone a paradigm shift. The buying experience is no longer linear.

Today's marketers need actionable strategies that provide a seamless brand experience for the customer, regardless of channel or device.

Think Dollar Shave Club's digital media trumpet, "Our Blades Are F***ing Great." Match a singular outrageous message to a singular audience segment as it did perfectly with 20-something men, and in a few short years you'll have a billion dollar shave club.

Or break the ties that bind your brand and prevent your brand from becoming who it really wants to be. History doesn't have to repeat itself. For years "We bring good things to life" brought good fortune to GE in revenue and recognition as one of the best slogans in recent marketing memory. But household appliance and lighting sales represented a small fraction of the company's burgeoning B2B business in digital industrial manufacturing. Rebrand with a multimedia story that shifts your product-centric narrative to emotionally captivating human experience, and you, too, can become a content marketing master with a new GE "Imagination at Work"- a campaign that wows. (And, by the way, a company that earns a highly engaged social media audience of 1.6 million Facebook followers.)

Or listen, really listen, to your audience and respond. Taco Bell did when it learned nearly 70% of its customers preferred custom orders, but were reluctant to hold up the line behind them in its fast-food chains (those self-aware Millennials). Disrupt the market with a mobile order app that takes customization to a new level and happily watch your sales rise.

You don't need to be a big company to gain traction with an audience, either. Consider the Orabrush tongue cleaner, a product with a wrinkle-your-nose "ewww" factor that no amount of traditional advertising could make sexy. The company ditched its $40,000 infomercial for a $500 "Bad Breath Test" video on YouTube that led to a social media audience in the hundreds of thousands. Guess what you'll find now at your local Walgreens or CVS?

Then there's InVision and its creative collaboration platform that eases the work of design-heavy product development for all kinds of companies. InVision has a blog. A blog with lots of devoted followers. A blog with the singular purpose of feeding the passion of the creative crowd with unique design inspiration, culture, and principles. A blog that truly gets its audience and keeps them coming back.

The point is, you want your audience to keep coming back. For brand strategists and marketing practitioners, today's top priority is understanding customers — their demands, interactions, diversity, devices, and technologies — all the while delivering the right message across the right touch-points at the right time with utmost discipline and consistency.

In the following pages, we'll outline the principles of DBE. We'll provide you with key approaches that fast-moving brands use to adapt — and thrive — with disciplined marketing programs that steal market share, guaranteed.

V. What is Digital Brand Engagement?

DBE is the discipline that makes sense of the complex marketing stack that the new generation of marketers must manage. It's a principle that was first introduced in 2008 by digital advertising agency L7 Creative, which saw consumers being directed more and more into digital spaces. L7 Creative predicted that, in the evolving digital space, the kind of prevalent advertising that interrupts user attention would become increasingly ineffective. And it has.

Together the principles of DBE detail an approach that replaces (or augments) traditional, one-way advertising messages aimed at audiences with strategies that build connections through creative two-way conversations with the audience. These conversations seek to truly engage customers and help them build a relationship with a brand.

Marketers continue to need more and more sophisticated approaches to hold the attention of their more-demanding audiences. DBE includes a disciplined set of principles that, when applied, can reinvent, grow and intimately connect and hold brands to their audience.

DBE redefines marketing for the modern digital era. Take a look at the American Marketing Association's definition of marketing:

"Marketing is the activity, set of institutions, and processes for creating, communicating, delivering, and exchanging offerings that have value for customers, clients, partners, and society at large."

Sounds a bit one-way, even authoritarian, doesn't it? DBE, on the other hand, acknowledges the far more democratic, participatory nature of the digital world. It could be defined as:

"The science and art of developing meaningful connections with an audience by leveraging online ecosystems and tools."

From using apps to monitoring social buzz; creating and launching influencer campaigns; building thought leadership with ebooks and creating lead nurturing campaigns — the full capabilities of the digital space (and more on the horizon) can become part of an effective DBE strategy.

With so many options, we want to bring order and discipline to this new type of digital marketing.

A small percentage of the most effective marketers have fully embraced some (but not all) of the principles of DBE and now reap the rewards in increased sales, customer loyalty, and brand value.

Wherever you are on this continuum, the goal of this book is to provide you with proven guideposts that will lead you toward developing a DBE strategy that truly moves the needle for your brand, sales, and business objectives.

Principle #1:
Know Your Audience — and Yourself

For many companies, marketing amounts to little more than shouting undifferentiated messages at an uninterested audience, hoping that with enough volume, the tiny percentage who respond will add up to increased sales. The practice is much like the guy or gal you meet at a networking event who's too busy telling you about themself to have a meaningful conversation.

Don't be that person. The most successful marketers are genuinely interested in what makes their audience tick. They pay attention and put effort into learning how they can create *real value for specific people* in ways that show they're listening.

What if your engagement were more like:

Figure 1.1 – A great brand resides at the intersection of the company and its audience. You have to know yourself, and your audience, to develop real and engaging conversations.

Knowing your audience is a process

Fostering real audience knowledge across all aspects of your marketing **and sales organization is not something you can accomplish in an hour or even a day.** It's not done in the boardroom, and it's not accomplished by just going with your gut, either. It's a disciplined process that begins with digging deep to define your target audience. It employs primary research (also known as talking to your customers), followed by thoughtful evaluation of that research to pin down their key values, beliefs, lifestyles, attitudes, and decision-making criteria — in other words, the things that impact their likelihood of engaging with your brand.

Getting to know your audience

1. Define your target audience.

Your definition should detail typical demographics (age, income, education, geography, etc.), but it should also include psychographics. At the beginning, your definition of the values and interests of your target audience will probably be a bit generic. That's ok. It will get better with time and familiarity. Start with what you know, but realize when you're making an assumption and be open to being surprised.

2. Spend time with them.

This part takes awhile. If you're part of an established company, you can shortcut this phase a bit by working closely with the people in your organization who interact directly with your customers. This doesn't mean salespeople alone. You should seek out customer service representatives and anyone else who spends a significant amount of time with your customer. If you're starting a new company, you'll need to do this work from scratch; but even in an established firm, it's critical to supplement your secondary research (e.g., talking to your salespeople) with primary research. Artificial approaches, such as focus groups or surveys, can be helpful; but there's also a lot to be said about simply spending time around people. Want to sell to surfers? You'll probably have to get your hair wet. Want to sell to cigar aficionados? Better build up a tolerance for smoky clubs.

3. Document what you've learned.

This is a highly underrated step. We often hear marketers say they know their target audience like the back of their hands, but ask them to share anything specific about that audience and they come up blank. Writing things down reinforces clear thinking. You'll want to preserve your strategy for future team members. You're going to do such a good job with your marketing strategy that your company will grow, right? At some point during all that expansion, there will be new staff who need to be brought up to speed. Developing simple, clear documentation, such as customer personas, is an easy way to build consistency and morale among not only your marketing and sales staff, but your whole team.

4. Continue to refine.

Knowing your customer isn't a one-time effort. Values change over time. Your product, market, and the larger global environment will evolve. You'll launch new products or services and find new audiences for them, so it's important to regularly re-examine what you think you know about your customer and update the documentation you've developed to keep it fresh and relevant.

Brand, know thyself

It takes real self-confidence to be a good listener and build strong relationships with other people. The same goes for a brand.

A brand that knows "who it is" will have the confidence to connect authentically with its target audience. A company (like a person) that is too eager to please will simply end up annoying the people with whom it most wants to connect.

No brand can be all things to all people, although some can't help themselves from trying. **Resist the temptation to overly complicate your brand story.** In 1984, a handful of mass market producers dulled the taste buds of beer consumers with a limited selection of domestic pale lagers. A spirited home brewer in Boston bottled his family's kitchen recipe and went door-to-door encouraging local bars and restaurants to try his craft brew. Why? Because Jim Koch simply loved beer. He wanted to offer something better, something more flavorful, to like-minded enthusiasts. His Samuel Adams craft beer led a micro-brew revolution and found a highly loyal following. How? As a company, Samuel Adams understood what it was about, and it showed. It stuck to its core competency as a company that makes quality craft brews simply "for the love of beer."

Stand by your brand's purpose, and recognize that a great brand is inversely proportional to its scope. A common misconception of marketers (and often the management teams to which they report) is that the goal of marketing is to appeal to the largest possible number of people. This approach, however, results in watered-down messages that get lost in the white noise and end up appealing to no one. Whatever the values you believe in as a brand, don't be afraid to share them. You'll find your true, lasting fans that way.

Defining your brand

Be inclusive.

To build a brand personality that represents your company, include as many diverse voices in the creation phase as you can. You don't have to use every idea, but incorporating more people into the process can ultimately lead to greater buy-in and group cohesion. If your brand personality is authentic internally, it'll be real to your audience.

Use stories and imagery.

There's a reason so many creative agencies ask questions such as, "If your company were a car / animal / etc., what would it be?" Metaphors and imagery represent powerful ways to encourage people to turn concepts, like values and beliefs, into something tangible and real.

Show it off!

Once you've articulated the values and beliefs that make up your core brand, it's vital to put these values on display – literally as well as figuratively. Posting visual reminders of your brand values prominently around your offices will support your team in living those values each day. **At L7 Creative we developed a visual tool called the Brand Blueprint that many companies use to reinforce their brand identity.**

P.S., you are not your audience

Your brand exists at the intersection of your company and your audience. Your company values must absolutely be a part of the company-customer relationship, but recognize they're only a part of it. Depending on the demographics of the target audience, it's common for marketers to promote a brand to people who are younger or older than they are, or who have different educational levels or fall into different income brackets.

A phenomenon of projecting one's values onto others can creep, however unwittingly, into marketing tactics; but it frequently pops up at the senior executive and management levels. If your management team members are 50-plus-year-old MBAs earning more than $200,000 per year, but your product is aimed at college students who live on ramen noodles, there's basically no chance that the same content or creative material could appeal to both of those groups.

At some point you'll be faced with a member of your management team who "just doesn't like" the new content or creative you've developed. It takes real discipline and guts to put something out there that you know your audience will love – even if you don't – because you've taken the time to get to know them. The effort will pay off.

Be brave and have faith in your brand. Even more importantly, educate the non-marketers in your organization. There's a little bit of magic in the ability to really put yourself in other people's shoes and see your content the way they would. Great marketers cultivate this ability over years in their trade, so it's not fair to expect your CFO or senior VPs to do this instinctively. Help them out, and you'll create a win-win-win for yourself, your team, and your brand.

Principle #2:
Give Your Audience a Reason to Engage

With more than 42 million Facebook pages and one billion-plus websites, the scale of the web is frankly unimaginable. Precisely where you land in this ever-expanding universe can be tough to pinpoint. In the past, the most significant brands faced a handful of competitors that they could realistically keep track of on an individual basis. Today you might compete not only with a few other well-known companies, but also with startups, offshoring companies, or SaaS substitutes for your service — and there may be thousands of them.

In this fast-moving environment, real brand engagement with your target customer is an incredibly valuable and scarce commodity.

At the same time, your customer is busier and their time is more fragmented than ever before. To secure those vital few minutes, or even seconds of their time, you'll need to contribute back to them in a thoughtful, strategic, and inventive way.

An effective DBE campaign is

REWARDING   **WELL POSITIONED**   **TIMELY**

Figure 2.1 – There are three major elements in an effective DBE campaign.

Reward your participants by avoiding Field-of-Dreams thinking

Most social promotions fail, at least in the sense that they don't return the level of engagement, sales, users, etc., for which a company hopes. A common reason for flops is assuming the "if you build it, they will come" mentality.

Having cleverly written and nice-looking social channels doesn't guarantee that people will actually engage with you. Even providing highly interactive elements (games, apps, and so on) doesn't mean people will actually interact with them.

American Honda Motor Co. held high hopes when they redirected their budget for cable TV ads to their own newly developed media properties. The Honda Stage concept, anchored by a website and YouTube channel, was designed to attract young drivers to Honda's Civic and Accord models with music videos filmed at company-sponsored events. The result didn't return the numbers or foster the engagement Honda anticipated.

"We thought that the website and YouTube channel would be a destination," Thomas Peyton, Honda's Assistant Vice President of Marketing, told the Wall Street Journal. "But that isn't how people want to use us."

Joe Pulizzi, founder of the Content Marketing Institute, tells the story of a workshop he hosted in late 2015 for CEOs representing a cross-section of American small business. Across plumbers, consultants, retailers and manufacturers, a theme emerged: "Our blog gets little traffic. No one likes our Facebook posts. Our e-newsletters don't convert."

Pulizzi asked the group a question too few marketers ask themselves: "Is the content you are creating and distributing for your customers any different than anything else out there?" The answers were predictable — the usual coupons and articles or videos regurgitated a million times, even by competitors. He followed up with the one question that should precede any discussion of digital content development: "Why should my customers care?"

An effective campaign plan invites people to join the conversation. It includes a call to action, an encouragement to motivate users to jump in. It gives potential participants an answer to the classic question, "What's in it for me?"

Common motivators for engagement

Tangible rewards aren't the only motivation for people to work for your brand; they're not even the best. The specific triggers for your audience will vary, but they can usually be grouped into a few categories:

a) Recognition: "I'll get a shout-out that improves my reputation."

b) Self-esteem: "I'll feel better about myself for getting involved."

c) Free stuff: "I get to try the new product for free."

d) Money: "I'll save, or earn, cold hard cash for participating."

Of course, motivators can be combined in any number of ways. Sending out a few pairs of a new shoe design to your Facebook fans before the line hits the market combines "free stuff" with "recognition." Participants gain insider status that makes them feel special. Involving your customers in a cause or organization you support — medical research, for example, or a disaster relief nonprofit — promote feelings of "recognition" and "self-esteem" among your audience that, in turn, promotes social media sharing. Remember the staggeringly successful, Internet-breaking Ice Bucket Challenge for ALS? A prime example of this concept.

Help them look and feel good

Beyond simply rewarding people for engagement, it's also vital that you consider the positioning of your campaign and how it relates to the digital environment.

The importance of self-image among consumers can't be understated, although it would be an exaggeration to say that with social media everyone has suddenly become a narcissist. On the other hand, there's no question that, due to the public nature of today's digital environment, people who might never use the phrase "personal brand" have become surprisingly adept at managing the way they look to others online.

The fact that many of the actions we take online essentially become permanent in Google history doesn't help us with anonymity, either.

It's vital that any online promotion be positioned in such a way that participation elevates the user in his or her own mind and in the minds of his or her peers.

Let's break the ties that bind your brand and keep you from being who you really are or want to be. History doesn't *have to* repeat itself. For years, "We bring good things to life," brought good fortune to GE in revenue and recognition as one of the best slogans in marketing history. But household appliance and lighting sales represented a small fraction of the company's burgeoning B2B channel in digital industrial manufacturing. Rebrand with a multimedia story that shifts your product-centric narrative to emotionally captivating the human experience, and you, too, can become a content marketing master with an "Imagination at Work"-like campaign that wows. (And, not to mention, a company that earns a highly engaged social media audience — 1.6 million Facebook followers, anyone?)

Scale vs. Engagement

REVENUE vs FANS

LUXOTTICA $9.7B

WARBY PARKER $1.2B

WARBY PARKER 500k

LUXOTTICA 57k

Figure 2.2 – Last year Luxottica earned enough revenue to beat Warby Parker eight times over, but Warby Parker beats them by more when it comes to online engagement.

Timeliness: Give them a reason to engage NOW

We're all busy. How many times have you seen a product or an offer and thought, "Sounds interesting. I'll follow up on that later." How many times did you actually do it?

In general, the offer we act on right away is the only one that really matters. To make your digital promotions effective, it's critical you give an "act now" imperative.

Sometimes a must-have angle is built into the nature of a promotion, such as a year-end sale, or an upcoming event with a specific date. If not, you'll need to create artificial urgency.

A few examples of ways to create urgency include:

It's all about the NOW

- Hold contests and set a date when the winner will be chosen.

- Set an expiration date for a one-time-only special offer.

- Determine an artificially low number of available spots in your promotion, as in: "This price is available only to the first 10 buyers," or "Only 25 seats left in our seminar."

No formula can guarantee that people will feel compelled to connect with your campaign. But by rewarding participants thoughtfully, positioning your brand to raise their self-esteem when they engage, and creating a sense of timeliness and urgency, you'll give yourself the best chance to launch a successful DBE program.

Principle #3:
Stand for Something

Don't be afraid to shout that you stand for something. Recognize that your brand can attract some people, and it can deter others. Great brands don't mind that. They know that being consistent, transparent, and bold gives the brand purpose.

Sure, you want your brand to reach the largest possible number of people; but be careful your message doesn't get sucked into a black hole of statistics. Overly broad messages designed to please the masses end up pleasing nobody. Your values make you unique. Be authentic and share them.

> **"** *If you stand for something, you will have people for you and people against you. But if you stand for nothing, you will have nobody for you and nobody against you"*
>
> — Maurice Saatchi

But let's be clear here: Very few brands (or people for that matter) would publicly announce that they don't want to stand for something or be bold. Yet those principles become real (or not) when they encounter the often messy domain known as real life.

In order to be successful in taking and maintaining a principled position in the marketplace, there are some basic disciplines you'll need, along with tools that help support them.

Be consistent

Cultures, like habits, are powerful. They can be hard to construct, but once built, they acquire momentum and can take on a life of their own. Shaping any habit is a matter of consistency.

Consistency begins by clearly stating the cultural values you want your company to embody. It's easy to overlook this. Many less experienced marketers and executives will say they have strong company values, but they will struggle to articulate them. Their junior staff might be even less aware of them.

If you've really put work into DBE Principle #1 ("Know your audience — and yourself"), you already have some ideas about what matters to both your team and your target customers. Translate these ideas into company principles or value statements.

Here are a few examples:

Define your values

Company Trait	Value statement
Environmentally sensitive	We are committed to sustainability in all our manufacturing practices.
Creative and edgy	We never settle for the status quo and always push the envelope on design and style.
Service-focused	We give five-star service in every customer interaction.

Figure 3.1 – Craft your value statement to describe the action in support of that particular company trait.

Good value statements are active and prescriptive. Many vision statements or mission statements fall short by limiting themselves to something like, "We believe X, Y, or Z." Believing something is ok, but what you do is what matters. Develop your value statements in terms of action.

Because value statements are prescriptive, they allow you to evaluate every aspect of your company against them whether that be an advertisement, a new product, a customer interaction, or a new hire. For instance, ask "When we did X, were we standing up for sustainability?" The ability to ask those questions empowers everyone on your team to enforce and raise the standards of the group in following your principles.

Once you've clearly articulated your values, you can begin to develop the habits that strengthen them.

Create consistency

- Develop a clear statement of your company's principles.

- Make the statement visible to everyone in the company.

- Enforce accountability by being public about your commitment to your values.

- Celebrate team members who demonstrate the application of company principles.

- Regularly evaluate your adherence to your company values.

- Name one or more of your team members as the gatekeeper, in which they guard the consistency of your company's voice and values across all platforms.

Be transparent

In the infinitely connected environment of digital and social media, it's not enough for your company's values to be articulated by the marketing and PR departments.

It might have been possible 20 years ago to project a facade to the public and do something totally different on the inside of a company, but those days are gone. With the near 100% penetration of social networks into businesses (not to mention the fact that nearly every employee carries a digital video camera on their smartphones 24/7), the only viable option is to be authentic.

The good news is that for companies willing to be consistent in applying their core values both inside and outside, there are tribes of potential customers who will reward this effort with increased engagement and loyalty.

Being transparent includes admitting your mistakes. No company is perfect, and in some cases how a company responds to a misstep can have a much more public impact than how they handle the mistake itself.

Even the best marketing plans can fall flat. When Invisible Children, a small nonprofit organization dedicated to assisting young victims of an ongoing conflict in East Africa, failed to meet a fundraising goal, it didn't skirt the issue with donors. Unprompted by anything other than its desire to be transparent, it posted a detailed blog about the under performance of its donation campaign describing why and how it intended to scale back some of its initiatives. It was a tough truth to broadcast, but the straight-up acknowledgment of the organization's challenges lifted the veil on its internal workings, brought donors into the decision-making process, and strengthened public trust.

Don't underestimate the power of customer service. Consider the classic video "United Breaks Guitars" that went viral back in 2008 (generating more than 10 million views almost immediately). Taking weeks to half-heartedly apologize to a customer who had his $3,500 Taylor guitar destroyed, ultimately cost United Airlines far more in negative brand impressions than in positive customer action. Compare this fail to JetBlue, consistently lauded as a top social media performer. JetBlue often responds in as little as six minutes to customer service tweets, and has generated huge amounts of earned media through its helpful responses.

The approach is no accident. According to an interview with Laurie Meacham, JetBlue's Manager of Customer Commitment, the company's Twitter account is managed collectively by its marketing, communications, and customer commitment groups. JetBlue makes a real effort to build a customer service model that takes into account all aspects of DBE in responding to customer issues. Quickly taking responsibility for issues and working to resolve them in the public forum of social media can ultimately boost your brand.

Be bold

Once you've defined your values and overcome the barriers in your organization that might prevent you from truly expressing them, it's time to get out into the public and make some noise. Being well behaved or playing by the rules is a losing strategy — especially if you're a startup company not yet established in the marketplace.

A bold message is not just unique; in many cases it can be uncomfortable, jarring, or unexpected. From classic campaigns like Volkswagen's "Think Small" to Burger King's bizarre "subservient chicken," defying expectations can be rewarded in a big way. This is even more apparent in digital media where capturing the zeitgeist, even briefly, can lead to game-changing results for a brand.

It can take a grand gesture to get the attention of the marketplace. Given the speed and transience of digital media, you may only have a slim window to make your message heard at precisely the time when it can make the biggest difference.

Capturing the greatest opportunities to engage with your audience requires not only being ready to seize the moment, but also being willing and empowered to do so.

Management teams that have not yet grasped the importance of DBE often make the mistake of requiring too many approvals and creating too much friction on the marketing team. This can lead to missed opportunities. Even worse, it can reduce the willingness of the marketing team to take risks or move quickly.

Oreo's classic "You can still dunk in the dark" tweet contemporaneously posted during the 2013 Super Bowl blackout created far more brand impressions than the actual commercial for which the brand paid for. Designed, executed, approved, and launched within the 36-minute blackout, this represents a great example of teamwork minus the friction of excessive management.

Build boldness

• Boldness starts at the top. Get your management team on board.

• Brainstorm regularly to keep your campaigns fresh.

• Lower barriers to approval. Be willing and able to quickly test new ideas.

• Be brave.

Authenticity, or lack thereof, can make or break a brand. Stand by your brand, reinforce it with consistency and transparency, and show some courage. Your customers will reward you with interest, engagement, and loyalty.

Principle #4:
Develop Discipline

" *We are what we repeatedly do. Excellence, then, is not an act, but a habit."*

— Aristotle

In our first three Principles of DBE, we've built the foundation of your brand and determined how you'll engage with your target audience. In this next step, you'll learn to adopt the habits necessary to ensure your foundation is not only maintained, but also used to build a powerful and lasting digital presence.

We've encouraged you to practice consistency in your DBE efforts. Achieving consistency is not just a matter of good copy editing and the topic deserves detailed discussion.

Consistency has always been a difficult virtue to maintain in an environment of constant change, where the demands on your marketing department are often massive and seem to shift with the wind. But the best brands have always been the ones that have managed to accomplish consistency in spite of its challenges —whether it's Coca-Cola, with its brand largely unchanged for well over 100 years, or Apple, with its strident commitment to a great design that has not only endured, but also pulled the company from its early-90s death spiral.

The challenges of consistency are even more pronounced in the environment of DBE, where change happens insanely fast, expectations are through the roof, and competition for the audience's attention is practically mind-boggling.

So how exactly does DBE consistency benefit your brand?

Consistency gets your message heard

Science says a pet goldfish has a longer attention span than your average customer. Thanks to smartphones and humans' seemingly limitless capacity to scroll, a study conducted by Microsoft showed our attention spans have fallen from 12 seconds in 2000 to 8 seconds today. The humble goldfish can hang onto information for a full second longer than we can.

And there's an ever-growing heap of competition for our limited focus, especially on social media channels. On Facebook alone, there's a whole lot of "liking" going on — every 60 seconds Facebook users react to 4 million posts, more than 349,000 tweets are generated, and Instagram photos score 1.7 million likes.

Let's look at those numbers in another way:

Figure 4.1 – Worldwide (in 1 hour), there are millions of Facebook likes, Instagram likes, and Tweets.

In a modern digital ecosystem that counts user engagement like astronomers count the stars, sending a message out just once is like yelling into the wind. Your message is gone before it even has a chance to make an impact.

If you want to be heard above a crowd, you don't just need to speak loudly – **you need to speak clearly, consistently, and frequently.** Even better, get a whole group to dependably holler along with you, and even the most attention-challenged or jaded listener will begin to take notice.

Consistency fosters trust

In a world of fake reviews, spam comments, and virtual companies that might or might not actually exist, trust is at an all-time premium.

Just as you trust a person more and more over time when he or she acts in a reasonably predictable way and displays consistent values, we trust companies more when their actions are consistent. Also, "consistent" doesn't have to mean "boring." We expect Bank of America ads to be full of platitudes about financial planning and saving for retirement. But we also expect Red Bull to throw a guy out of a plane at the edge of space and Kanye to rant on Twitter. It's the consistency that builds the trust.

In DBE, it's especially important to put this trust in the context of the "sharing" relationship. After all, if someone likes your Facebook page, follows you on Twitter, or reviews your product on Amazon, they're sending a message to their friends, family, and even acquaintances that says they believe in your brand and stand behind it. They won't do that if your messaging is so unpredictable that they're afraid of what you'll say next — whether it's inappropriate, out of touch, or downright embarrassing. It takes substantial trust to become a brand ambassador, to make a stand for a product or company, and trust builds on trust. People are much more likely to share content that has already been shared by their friends.

How does this translate in DBE? It happens at every step in the engagement process and across every channel.

- When clicking your ad takes the visitor to a landing page that matches the ad, you build trust.

- When images on your Facebook page looks similar to ones on your website, you build trust.

- When your content has a style and tone that readers come to recognize, you build trust.

- When the follow-up emails you send remind recipients of the content they read on your site before signing up, you build trust.

- And so on, and so on.

Consistency builds your story over time

A great story evolves over time; it isn't static. The story's characters must be consistent enough for the audience to identify with them and become invested in their destinies. The same is true for your brand.

Maintaining core values, such as innovation, high design, and a hefty dose of snobbishness, has helped Apple to build a great story that took it from a humble newcomer in the desktop computer industry to a global leader in personal technology. This evolution was actually by no means an obvious one; it seems so only in retrospect. Why would a computer company create a music player anyway? Yet coming from Apple as part of an ongoing story of transformation that led from the iMac to the iPod, the narrative was not only believable, but it also felt safe.

By contrast, without good storytelling and consistent brand values, new brand extensions can fall horribly flat. Witness the Zune, Microsoft's own painful effort to join the portable music player market and win back some of the ground it lost to Apple. At its peak during the 2008 holiday season, the Zune generated $85 million for Microsoft versus the iPod's $3.37 billion. One way to look at this flop is that the Zune story didn't give consumers a reason to trust Microsoft to make a great music player. The company didn't craft a consistent story as a lifestyle brand the way that Apple had.

Why is consistency so hard?

It seems reasonable to expect that if you study your audience and create a good brand position, as we've discussed in the earlier DBE Principles, then the rest takes care of itself. Unfortunately, it isn't so easy, your brand doesn't stay on course without constant energy inputs.

In physics, this energy-input process is called entropy, which roughly translates to the reality that order **always breaks down into disorder over time unless more energy is added to the system.** "Energy" in our marketing world represents the continuous effort by disciplined marketers to keep the company on-message and ensure teams work together.

But you might reasonably wonder what it is that you're pushing against when you exert all this effort? In other words, what erodes thoughtful planning and organization you're building to keep your company on track?

It most likely isn't a bunch of nasty co-workers who are secretly (or even not-so-secretly) working to sabotage your planning and projects. In all likelihood, the people who break down your carefully developed plans have only the best of intentions.

It's critical to understand that organization and production are often at odds, particularly in a fast-moving enterprise. In other words, the continuous efforts to "get stuff done" or "get the project out the door" tend to unwittingly obliterate planning and policy.

- The advertisement that needs to go to press in four hours, so there's no time to have someone check it against the brand book.

- The website that gets built by a different agency because your usual guys that know your brand inside-and-out are busy on another project.

- The trade show booth that basically gets designed by the sales guys because marketing is too slammed with other projects.

These and a thousand similar occurrences, day in and day out, are the elements that wear down the order you're working to build. And since the people doing this stuff are not evil, (usually) taking vengeance on them just seems mean. After all, they're "just trying to get the work done!"

What's the missing ingredient in these scenarios, you might ask, that would stave off the forces of entropy and ensure a consistent brand, even when the going gets tough? The answer may be boring, but it's true. The solution to creating consistency in spite of all these challenges?

One thing alone: Discipline.

What is brand discipline in DBE?

Brand discipline could be defined as:

The consistent application of your brand's style, tone, and values to all communications in every medium.

This discipline gets particularly tested in the accelerated environment of DBE, where there simply isn't time to run everything up the flagpole for approval by brand managers.

Without the enforced, automatic discipline of publication deadlines and hard-copy proofs to approve, it takes more forethought to maintain brand standards.

Here are the five key steps to follow in creating brand discipline for DBE:

1. **Document.** First, you can't enforce a standard that doesn't exist. Work with your team to document the key values of your brand.

2. **Simplify.** Boil down the key truths of your brand into a tight enough format that everyone in your organization can actually commit them to memory as if they're second nature.

3. **Visualize.** Post these simplified, clarified values prominently and ensure they are constantly being seen by your team. If team members have to dig out the 34-page brand book every time they compose a tweet, you've already lost the battle.

4. **Reinforce.** Periodically refresh your team's understanding of your brand values. Don't just call people out for violating a rule. Instead, celebrate innovative content or posts that embody the best in your brand.

5. **Explain why.** Give your people credit for wanting to do the right thing. Especially for young novice marketers, brand guidelines can seem constricting and Orwellian. Educate your team on the DBE principles in this ebook so they understand that following the guidelines is part of a bigger picture that creates real value.

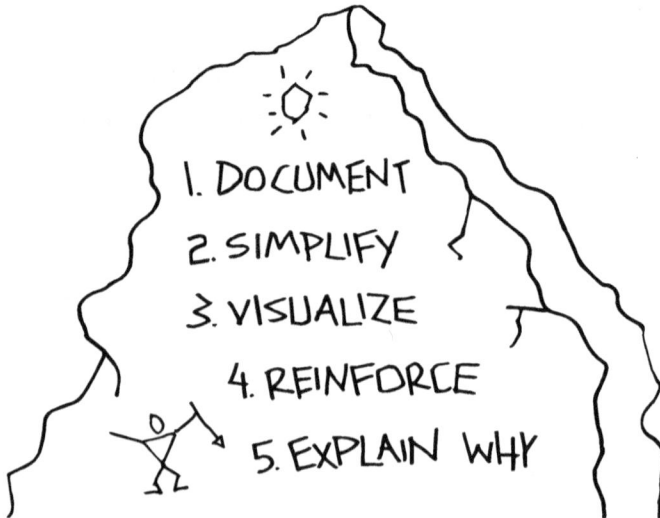

Figure 4.2 – Follow these five steps to achieve brand discipline.

By following these steps, you can open the door to consistent implementation of your brand across all your DBE channels. This will increase your visibility in a crowded space; create trust with your audience so they will share; and ultimately allow you to build a story over time that truly elevates your brand.

Achieving this consistency across a team of marketers requires substantially more planning and effort than you might think. In Principle #5, we'll dig into ways to keep your team coordinated across various disciplines.

Principle #5:
Work Collaboratively Across Disciplines

One of the most challenging aspects of managing a modern brand is the sheer breadth of media options available. Each option requires its own tactical execution, not to mention diverse training and management. This challenge becomes greater as a brand grows and the marketing team naturally increases in both size and specialization.

Yet the need for coordination across these teams has never been more important.

A DBE strategy can involve a dozen disciplines.

Figure 5.1 – Several factors must be taken into account to coordinate your DBE disciplines.

Depending on the size of your organization, these disciplines might all be handled by one or two (very overworked) in-house staff; they might be split among a large group of internal specialists; or they could be divided between your staff and an agency or agencies. **In every case, information, results, analytics, and trends must be coordinated** between disciplines to achieve a consistent brand story and effective optimization of your DBE campaigns.

A marketer who takes DBE seriously, must **develop effective strategies for breaking down silos, promoting cross-pollination of ideas, and helping the best approaches rise to the top** and spread across the marketing organization.

In "Principle #4: Develop Discipline", we addressed how critical it is for a brand to communicate a stable message over time. An additional challenge emerges when multiple departments and stakeholders develop their own "versions" of your campaign. To avoid this predicament, you need to learn the silos and how you can break them down.

Information silos: Not just for Fortune companies

One of the most surprising things L7 Creative has found in working with hundreds of organizations — from established international corporations to fast-growing startups — is that big corporations do not have a monopoly on information silos and coordination failures. We've interviewed teams of executives who work in the same room and who still express strikingly different statements of their company's elevator pitch or positioning.

Of course, it's just as difficult to maintain information flow in a big connected group as it is between fully siloed groups, but disconnects can happen anywhere and at any time.

- Product teams that don't talk to one another but remain focused on their own product and numbers

- Customer service that fails to share with marketing all of the great (or not-so-great) feedback received through customer interactions

- SEO teams that don't communicate with social media content teams to ensure all of the content that each team produces is coordinated around the same keyword goals

- PPC teams that don't think to share insights gained through landing page campaigns with web development teams to improve website conversions

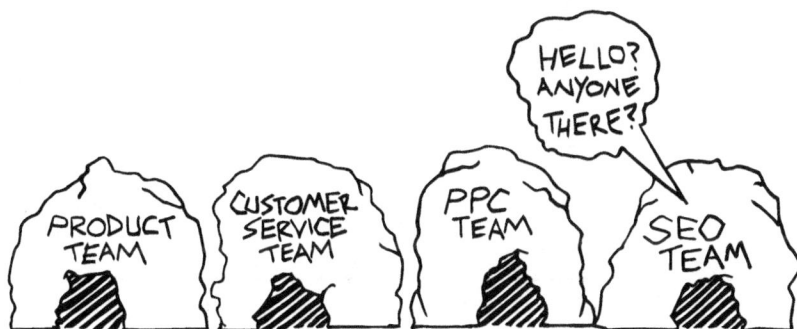

Figure 5.2 — Unfortuantely, disconnects can occur between silos when they can't, or won't, communicate effectively.

There are, of course, 1,001 variations on these scenarios. The end result? Serious wasted effort that reduces the power and reach of an organization's communication tactics.

The solution? Developing a disciplined habit of breaking down silos.

Why would smart people act this way?

Silos are often defined as a reluctance by one department or sector to share information with others within the same company. This is actually an incomplete definition.

In reality, silos are more often the result of a few factors that run rampant in today's workplace. In many ways they're not the fault of the team themselves.

Silo Source	Silo-Breaking Solution
Overwork and overwhelm. Let's face it: Everyone is too busy. Despite numerous studies showing that shorter work days can be more productive, working around the clock is practically America's national pastime. One result of all this burning-the-candle-at-both-ends is people tend to put their heads down and charge through a never-ending to-do list. The thing that often gets dropped out? Really connecting with colleagues.	Build collaborative time into your schedule. This doesn't mean you should wander up to your coworkers at random (they're busy, too!). Instead, block out a spot on your calendar for a routine meeting with each of the key people (even in other departments) with whom you can synergize efforts. Spending even one hour a week in a focused meeting can prevent misfires or duplicated effort.
	Get control of your workload by creating a "don't do" list. Identify actions that don't add much value, and cut down on them to make time for reflection and coordination with other people in your organization.

Figure 5.3 – There are various sources that may lead to disconnected silos. Luckily, they are also silo-breaking solutions.

Silo Source	Silo-Breaking Solution
Lack of a management imperative for collaboration. It's remarkable the degree to which people will follow the path of least resistance. Put all the programmers in one office, and they will rarely talk to the designers next door. Why? They're all the way next door. Management that doesn't build an imperative for communication across disciplines contributes to communication problems.	**Make silo-breaking a part of your culture.** Integrate the staff — consciously set up your office space to **put people of different disciplines in close proximity.** Create weekly **lunch-and-learn meetings** in which people from around your organization can learn about the work of their colleagues.
Emphasizing efficiency over effectiveness. "There is surely nothing quite so useless as doing with great efficiency what should not be done at all." — Peter Drucker Many companies have embraced specialization as a way to create greater efficiency. If one guy or gal handles just Facebook and another handles only Twitter, they'll both get faster and faster at it, right? Sure. Meanwhile, this approach doubles the effort involved in keeping your brand voice consistent across social channels. More efficiency is achieved, but what really matters — effectiveness — is reduced.	**Follow the Pareto Principle (a.k.a. the 80/20 rule)** You get about 80% of your results from about 20% of your efforts. This is especially true of activities that have the potential for exponential growth, such as DBE. **Identify key influencers, trends, and opportunities. Then share them with everyone in your organization who they can impact.** This will help you generate more result with less effort. A simple weekly staff meeting or even an email that **outlines trends and highlights successful actions** by your top-producing marketers can be a game changer for organizational effectiveness. For extra points, read Drucker's **The Effective Executive.**

Figure 5.3 – There are various sources that may lead to disconnected silos. Luckily, they are also silo-breaking solutions.

Keys to effective collaboration

While these silo-busting solutions will help to make space (both literally and figuratively) for more effective communication, real collaboration is a skill set all its own.

- **Be curious.** Changing the lens through which you view your work represents one of the most powerful things that can happen when you collaborate. Whether it's bringing a copywriter's sense of story to a visual design, or a programmer's systematic approach to a content strategy problem, when we collaborate we learn more about others, not to mention ourselves. Be an active listener, ask questions, and be there to learn. By the way, doing so can also lead to greater organizational effectiveness. For example, it's common for a web developer to hit a snag when implementing a design. A siloed approach would have them asking their coworker or supervisor for help making the design happen, without asking why, and burning many hours in the process. A silo-breaking approach would have them meet with the designer and become curious about the goal of the design. Our more engaged developer in this scenario would then collaboratively develop a design and code solution that's not only quicker to implement, but also achieves shared goals.

- **Be respectful.** We all remember the lunchroom in high school that was aggressively self-segregated between the geeks, the jocks, the skateboarders, the cheerleaders, etc. Segregation (even when it's self-imposed) can breed contempt, including among otherwise reasonable people. Sales hates on marketing because marketing just "makes pretty pictures all day" while sales actually makes it rain. Web developers hate on designers for putting drop shadows on everything and on the project manager for agreeing to everything the boss requests. You get the picture. Humans beings are naturally tribal, and that's okay to an extent. No one is asking the sales guys to put up Star Wars posters to be more like the developers, but management has a responsibility to keep everyone working together with mutual respect.

- **Be positive.** It's always easier to tear down someone else's idea than to build up your own. Encourage teams to provide positive feedback where they can and to make all criticism constructive. While the compliment sandwich is a bit played out, it's nonetheless true that people can shut down if all they hear is criticism. There's almost always something to like in someone else's work. Find it, and reinforce it.

- **Be goal-oriented.** Collaboration works best when we have mutual goals. Setting these goals at the beginning of a discussion or meeting (whether formally or informally) helps to ensure that the discussion stays productive. Whenever disagreements arise, or when there are multiple suggestions on ways to address an issue, goal-setting provides an opportunity to re-frame the discussion in terms of stated objectives and desired outcomes. Be sure you leave a meeting with clearly articulated next steps. Don't be afraid to ask, "Okay, so what are our action items here?"

A word on collaborative software

Just as a great tennis racket will not make you Serena Williams, no piece of software is going to make your group collaborative. There are some tools that can help if they are implemented thoughtfully.

- **Use channels and chat rooms wisely.** Tools such as Slack and Basecamp allow the creation of channels, where teams can come together to discuss a project or topic. These tools can be overwhelming if they're misused. A good approach is to "graze" from time to time on information contained in channels that aren't your immediate priority, rather than trying to read every post all the time. By quickly skimming through these channels, you can pick up a lot of the general trend of a project without committing too much time to it, helping to ensure you don't get blind-sided by a new development that suddenly hits your department.

- **Reply-all liberally (at least within your organization).** Yes, this approach can create a lot of email; but if you follow good email management habits (such as clearing your inbox at specific times each day), you can keep an eye on a lot of activities without having to really invest time in them. Just as with channels and chat rooms, you can develop a talent for quickly scanning for information that's relevant to you. While there's a tendency to think it's more efficient to include fewer people in a communication, chances are you'll end up having to go back and fill people in with in-person meetings that eat up even more time. There's an important corollary to this, however: If you're building a culture of inclusion in which many people are copied on email chains, you must also train your team to only provide input when it's really necessary and adds value. Be respectful of other people's inboxes; just because you're copied on an email doesn't mean you should respond, especially if you don't have something critical to add.

- **Collaborative documents are your friends.** Collaborative document tools, such as Google Apps and Dropbox, represent other surprisingly underutilized resources. Virtually everyone uses these tools from time to time; but when you really make them a part of your workflow, magic happens. Need approval on a memo? Put it in a Google doc and allow a manager to make one or two edits and approve it immediately. Behold! Changes tracked and no version issues! This is usually a far more clear approach than emailing a document and getting written feedback in the body of an emailed reply. The reply is often ambiguous and requires more back-and-forth to get all that you need nailed down.

By setting good ground-rules for collaboration, developing a culture of silo-breaking, and choosing your systems wisely, your organization will be set up for faster and more complete implementation of your DBE program.

Principle #6:

Set Goals, and Measure
the Right Things

M ost established companies have some form of goal-setting and goal management in place. Surprisingly few, however, create accurate marketing goals.

Maybe your organization does a good job of setting goals for sales/revenue, operating budgets or gross profits.

On the other hand, marketing goals are often vague, ill-defined or even nonexistent. Compounding the problem is something frequently missed on the goals list to begin with: Digital marketing can play a colossal role in ensuring goals are achieved.

Quality DBE campaigns set both quantitative and qualitative goals.

Quantitative goals

These are the goals that are most easily measured through analytics tools. **It's imperative to benchmark each of the factors you measure** so that you can make before-and-after comparisons and monitor your progress over time.

The specific metrics should vary for any given campaign or situation, but some of the best indicators of increasing brand engagement include:

- Time on Site
- Page Views per Visit
- Returning Visitors
- Search Queries
- Non-branded Organic Search Visits
- Branded Search Visits
- Direct Traffic
- Conversion Rates
- Email Open Rates
- Email Click Rates
- Social Shares / Likes

Metric	Importance
Time on Site: The amount of time an average visitor spends on your website	In most cases, this is a good indicator that visitors find your content useful and interact with it **Measurement Tool(s):** Google Analytics, Adobe Analytics
Page Views per Visit: The number of pages an average user visits	Similar to Time on Site, higher Page Views per Visit can indicate that users are exploring your site and browsing more content **Measurement Tool(s):** Google Analytics, Adobe Analytics
Returning Visitors: The number of visitors who make a return trip to your site in a given time interval	This reveals whether your lead nurturing and/or retargeting efforts are paying off by bringing people back to your site **Measurement Tool(s):** Google Analytics, Adobe Analytics
Search Queries: The number of people searching for relevant terms who actually see your content in search results; a precursor to organic search visits	This tracks how well your site ranks in searches as a result of your SEO and social efforts **Measurement Tool(s):** Google Analytics
Non-Branded Organic Search Visits: The number of visitors arriving to your site from searches of general interest in your category	This type of visit shows whether you're succeeding in SEO and targeting a good selection of keywords **Measurement Tool(s):** SEO management tools such as Moz, Ahrefs, Linkdex
Branded Search Visits: The corollary to Non-Branded Organic Search Visits, measures the number of visitors who search for you by name	Improved Branded search numbers are indicative of effective remarketing campaigns, branding campaigns, and social efforts **Measurement Tool(s):** SEO management tools such as Moz, Ahrefs, Linkdex

Figure 6.1 – Track and analyze these metrics to measure your DBE efforts.

Metric	Importance
Direct Traffic: The number of visitors who directly type your site URL into their browsers	Improved Direct Traffic often results from effective retargeting, branding campaigns, and social media **Measurement Tool(s):** Google Analytics, Adobe Analytics
Conversion Rates: The percentage of traffic that makes its way to each successive step of your funnel (more on funnels later)	This tracks how effectively you're moving prospects through your marketing funnel **Measurement Tool(s):** Web analytics products (Google, Adobe), as well as CRM and marketing automation products (Salesforce, Infusionsoft, Marketo)
Email Open Rates: The percentage of people who open each email message or campaign	Improved Email Open Rates may represent an up-tick in list quality, improved email content, and effective subject lines **Measurement Tool(s):** Email marketing software (Mailchimp, Constant Contact, Campaign Monitor) and marketing automation software (Infusionsoft, Marketo, Pardot)
Email Click Rates: The percentage of people receiving your emails who click through to your site from a link within the email	Improved click rates indicate high quality email content and effective CTAs (call to actions) **Measurement Tool(s):** Email marketing software (Mailchimp, Constant Contact, Campaign Monitor) and marketing automation software (Infusionsoft, Marketo, Pardot)
Social Shares / Likes: The number of people who either "like" or "share" your content on social channels	Improved social metrics suggest that your content is interesting to your target audience and giving them a reason to engage with your brand **Measurement Tool(s):** Social Platforms (Facebook, Twitter, etc.); Social Management Tools (Hootsuite, sendible)

Figure 6.1 - Track and analyze these metrics to measure your DBE efforts.

Qualitative goals

By definition, qualitative goals are harder to measure and report, but they're nonetheless important to form a full picture of your DBE efforts.

Some typical areas of qualitative measurement include:

- Brand awareness
- Brand reputation
- Tone and attitudes on social media (Note: efforts are being made to quantify this, but it remains an emerging field for the time being.)

It's important to interview stakeholders, customer touch points (e.g., sales, customer service), distributors or partners, and end-user customers before, during, and after the launch of DBE campaigns. Doing so will allow you to track how your DBE programs impact perceptions and attitudes in the marketplace.

Making your goals SMART

First referenced in 1981 by George T. Doran in an article for Management Review, the concept of "SMART" goals has become commonplace in many successful firms. A number of formulations of these goals exist, but we've found the following version — which identifies the five characteristics of a SMART goal and examples for DBE — to be most effective:

- **Specific** – The goal is capable of being clearly articulated.

- **Measurable** – The goal can be tracked using metrics. It should be unambiguous whether this goal was met or not.

- **Assignable** – This outcome can be owned by a specific person. The person should be empowered as needed, including with appropriate budgets, to achieve the goal.

- **Realistic** – It must be reasonable to believe this goal can be achieved. This objective includes the availability of personnel and budgets to accomplish it.

- **Time-stamped** – A deadline should be established for meeting the goal.

SMART

SPECIFIC   MEASURABLE   ASSIGNABLE   RELEVANT   TIME-STAMPED

Figure 6.2 — Spending extra time to create goals that satisfy these elements will be worth it in the end.

Here's a not-too-SMART goal that might sound familiar to many:

"Increase our effectiveness in social media"

Here's a SMARTer formulation that gives the marketing team something they can really get going with:

"By the end of Q4 of this year, our content marketing team will increase social traffic to our web properties by 25%."

Formulating your goals using the SMART criteria is beneficial for several reasons:

- First, it ensures that everyone in the organization remains on the same page about what you want to achieve.

- Second, it helps to weed out unrealistic or poorly thought-out goals.

- Third, particularly in organizations with management teams that are unsophisticated in marketing tactics, demanding SMART goals epitomizes a powerful way to protect marketers from arbitrary or unrealistic goals that can damage morale and create friction between marketing and other departments, such as sales.

Remember, to be effective in DBE, get SMART about your goals!

Socializing your goals

Once you've defined your goals, it's vital they be communicated across the organization, not only within the marketing team, but to sales, management, and support departments, as well. It's all too common, especially in nimble organizations, to find that goals are not synchronized from one area to the next. This can lead to missed expectations and tremendous frustration.

You might be familiar with these examples of the headaches that evolve from out-of-sync goals:

- Marketing targets 1,000 leads this quarter. Sales, on the other hand, projects 250 sales. Yet the historical conversion rate has only been 15%.

- Customer service needs one staff member per 100 customers, but marketing projects 500 new customers this year. No one has informed customer service that it should recruit five new staff to keep up with demand.

- Management has given the board a projection of 50% growth this year, but the advertising and marketing budget model would predict only 15% growth.

Figure 6.3 – Communicate your goals throughout your organization to ensure they match up from department to department.

Think of your organization as a large, complex machine, such as an automobile with multiple sub-systems that interrelate. If you regularly visualize your organization this way, it'll be easy to see there's seldom a time at which a decision about one area doesn't impact other areas down the line. If the design team adds six inches to the wheelbase of your car, for instance, it'll become clear that you'll need to inform the team building the chassis to accommodate those additional inches. But you'll also need to update the body panels. You'll need longer brake cables. The weight distribution will have to be reviewed by the safety team, and so forth.

The same applies to an organization and its marketing goals. It's quite common for sales goals and marketing budgets to be created by two different executives with little coordination between them; yet there are perhaps no two aspects of performance in an organization that are more tightly correlated. (Budgeting is another contender here and is discussed in more detail below.)

As Peter Drucker points out throughout *The Effective Executive*, the results of an organization are always found outside the organization. In other words, results mean those things the organization exchanges with its customers, the community, the world. And the activity that most directly impacts this exchange? Marketing, of course.

Marketing goals are not only the business of the marketing department. They are intimately concerned with everything the organization is doing. That means whatever the organization is doing — product development, public relations, recruitment, and more — should ultimately be coordinated with branding and marketing efforts in order to maximize an organization's productivity.

Defining your funnels

A crucial aspect of measuring your DBE efforts includes documenting and understanding your funnels, that is, the steps prospective customers take as they move from unawareness of your service to awareness and all the way through to making a purchase.

In a well-crafted DBE program, five or more steps typically define the funnel process. Multiple funnels can exist; in reality there could be one funnel for every marketing channel, depending on the complexity of your program.

Many naive marketing organizations measure at best one or two conversion rates, such as "web visitors to sales." Such a blunt metric is better than nothing, but it actually doesn't give the marketing team much ability to optimize. There can be any number of reasons for an improvement or decline in the metric, so it can be difficult to determine the cause of a change or propose solutions to create continuous improvement.

A comprehensive DBE program would include a series of funnels. Something like this:

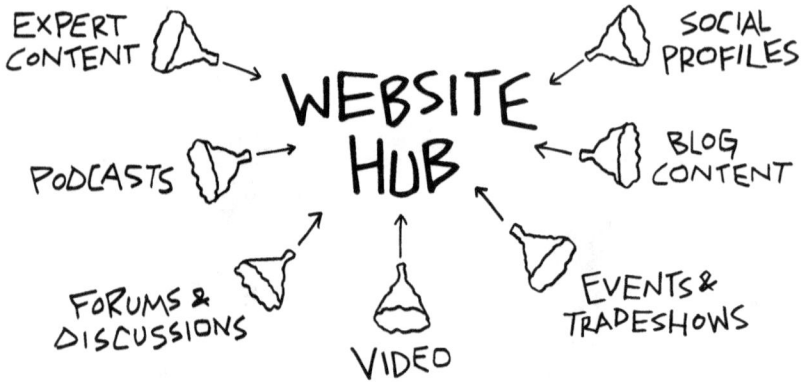

Figure 6.4 – Pay attention to the various funnels that lead to customer awareness.

As you can see, separate funnels can be employed for each of these marketing efforts, all of which drive traffic to a central website hub. Each funnel can then move forward into a sales conversion process.

Here's an example funnel that many marketing departments have in place:

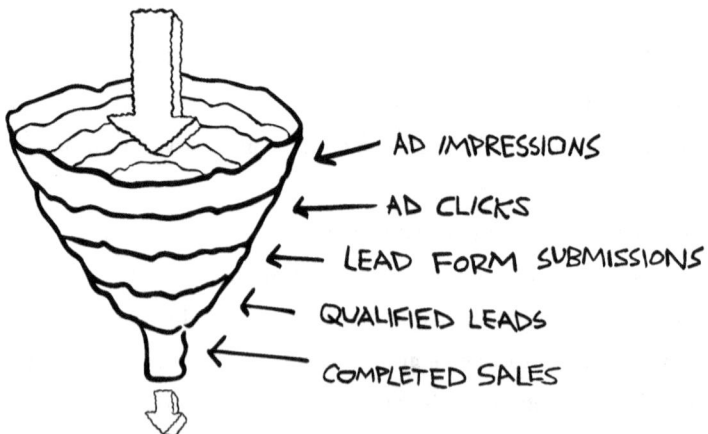

Figure 6.5 – This is a typical funnel that illustrates the journey your customers take, leading to a sale.

An individual funnel for digital advertising is pretty easy to define; it's the one we most often think of as a "funnel." To help broaden our view, let's take a look at a more interesting example for blog content:

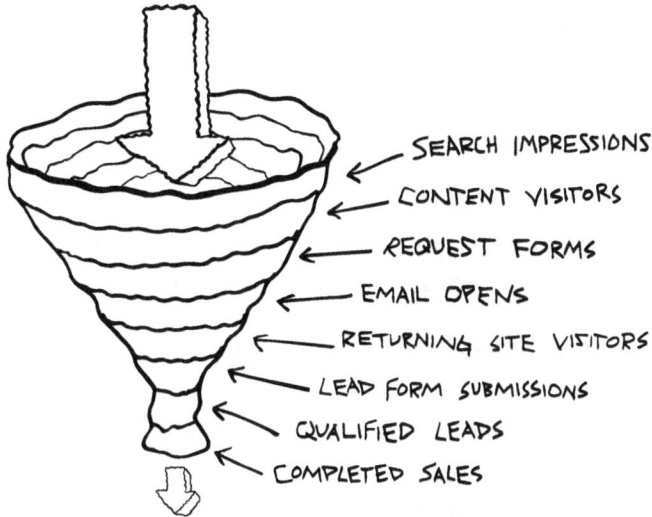

Figure 6.6 — A funnel for blog content may not be as straightforward, but provides valuable information.

Similar funnels can be developed for each facet of your DBE programs. As a first step, realize that every person who has become aware of your brand is somewhere in a funnel, and there is always a next action they should be encouraged to take.

Developing, managing, and reporting on a series of well-defined funnels represents a key discipline that will lead to improved results across all your marketing efforts.

A word on budgeting

An effective DBE plan must **lock DBE-driven revenue goals to DBE budgets** for several reasons:

- **It ensures the targets set for DBE are realistic.** If your firm generated $10 million from digital marketing last year, and the goal is to generate $50 million this year, it's reasonable to expect close to a five-fold increase in the budget. Efficiency gains are great, but it's common for management teams to assume efficiencies will be realized without having any actual strategy in place to accomplish them. As a marketer you must resist this pressure. It generally leads to missed goals and frustration from your team.

- **DBE is highly vulnerable to "Field-of-Dreams" thinking.** Unsophisticated marketers often assume that simply creating a campaign and putting it online will lead to increased performance numbers. This is usually not the case. The majority of campaigns that reach big audiences include a substantial portion of paid media and promotional budgets.

- **DBE rests at the top of the funnel.** Digital campaigns generally reach the broadest audience, but they begin with the least engaged audience. Your objectives include developing and nurturing engagement among the audience to create sales. As most campaigns lose some volume at each step in the funnel, it's very easy to underestimate the amount of traffic you need to put in at the top to get out the sales numbers you need at the bottom.

By developing clearly articulated goals of both the qualitative and quantitative varieties, building the right funnels to monitor progress on these goals, and setting budgets appropriate to the goals, you'll be well on your way to running DBE campaigns that truly move the needle for your company.

Principle #7:
Periodically Calibrate
and Reset

While this may be the final principle of DBE, it's the one that really makes all the others work. As you build community, drive engagement, and even engage in battle with your competitors across the web, it's critical to periodically review your progress against your goals. Look at them across all of the other principles we've covered, and make the appropriate course corrections to stay on track.

What does it mean to calibrate and reset?

Calibrate is literally defined as:

To correlate the readings of (an instrument) with those of a standard in order to check the instrument's accuracy.

In the case of a DBE program, calibration means:

To compare the data you're getting (i.e., analytics, performance, qualitative and quantitative results) with the goals you've established in order to check the effectiveness of your DBE efforts.

Calibration also implies that before making a new test, trying a new strategy, etc., it's crucial to check all of your measurements. You need to know your benchmarks for your most important KPIs so you can accurately say whether a new approach is generating improvements.

Unlike calibrating a thermostat to a thermometer (known standard), you're calibrating a DBE campaign against ever-changing, dynamic benchmarks. That's where the "reset" part comes in.

From time to time it's crucial to:

- Reset your goals based on performance to date

- Reset your expectations based on new industry benchmarks

- Reset your timelines based on changing team dynamics and resources

And so on. This list varies from one company to another but the principle is the same.

Building the habit

The best way to implement calibration in your organization is to schedule it out. Ensure that routine reporting is developed for all of the KPIs you follow, and meet periodically to review it.

Here are a few key ways in which successful DBE marketers build the habit of consistent calibration and continuous improvement:

- **Use the important data.** You can track a million data points, but most people can only really think with a handful of them. Fine-tune what you're measuring so that you're focused on things you can impact and that make a visible difference in the organization. Don't worry if the KPIs you follow evolve over time.

- **Report on all KPIs at least once per month.** Share them with management even if they yawn at you. Especially if they yawn at you.

- **Graph your KPIs.** Individual data points ("up 15% over last month") fade into obscurity immediately. You're looking for trends, and those can only be seen on a graph. By "graph" we also mean "graph and post where someone can see it." Nothing creates accountability (or protects against management interference) like seeing performance data in black and white.

- **Look for correlations.** Become an expert at spotting how smaller individual statistics add up to make bigger ones. For example, "Every time we have an up-tick in leads, it's followed by an up-tick in sales about four weeks later." Or, "Every time we create a Facebook post celebrating our top-performing staff, we get an increase in incoming resumes."

- **Use your calendar.** Regularly reporting to management makes your calendar work for you and builds good habits. Scheduling pre-defined blocks of time each day, week, and month for reviewing performance data can help to ensure that reviews actually happen.

What does it mean when the data doesn't match up?

Everyone was so confident that the new strategy was going to be a hit and finally move your market share from 4% to 8%. Instead, you've dropped to 3%. What's a marketer to do? Clearly the new strategy isn't working. On the other hand, maybe that's not the case.

A decent, well-implemented strategy will beat a brilliant, unimplemented strategy every time.

Before you blame the strategy, it's imperative to conduct a truly rigorous test of the implementation:

- Was the program carried out according to plan?

- Did it get all of the resources (personnel, time, budget) that it was supposed to receive?

- Were the goals of the plan SMART goals or just wild speculation? (See "Principle #6: Set Goals and Measure the Right Things")

- Did irrelevant ideas get added into the program that changed its focus or made it confusing? (Programs that get worked on by a committee are particularly vulnerable to this one.)

- Is the data trending in the right direction, even if the goal was missed?

We apply one process to all DBE campaigns and optimizations, from the smallest tweak to a full back-to-the-drawing-board reboot:

1. If performance is weak, check the implementation of the current strategy.

2. If the strategy is not being fully implemented, implement it.

3. If the strategy is being implemented fully, but performance is still not improving, only then change the strategy.

Being fast vs. being right

If there's one core reality of the digital marketing space, it's that things move fast. And in many cases, fast is good. Getting ahead of emerging trends in your demographic; launching a product campaign in time for a key selling season; capturing the zeitgeist with the right piece of content at the right time — these things can propel a brand to new heights very quickly.

At the same time, the sheer speed of digital marketing means that course corrections need to be made more frequently and more thoughtfully. Being a few degrees off course in a covered wagon might land you a mile or two off course; a few degrees off with a Mars mission and — best case — you could end up in the middle of deep space. And since (thanks to Google) the web has an essentially infinite memory, some kinds of missteps can haunt you for quite a while.

Perhaps no channel entices the undisciplined marketer with the need for speed more — or offers more face-palm moments — than social media. The good folks at the Rhode Island Commerce Corporation probably won't forget showcasing footage of Iceland in a tweeted promotional video anytime soon (oops!), and neither will critics. Budweiser and Bloomingdales had some making up to do for cringe-worthy campaigns that stirred the social pot with what some people thought were inferences of date rape. And one has to wonder about the fate of the U.S. Department of Justice staffer who mistook a personal Twitter account for a professional one and accused CNN of trolling.

To a certain extent, the hyperactive velocity in the digital world also breaks our simple homo sapien brain. We evolved in cultural environments where change happened over a scale of hundreds or even thousands of years, so we're not hard-wired to handle the pace of change in today's environment. One response to this fundamental discomfort is to just put one's head down and charge forward blindly. If you've ever tried this strategy in any sport for example, you probably realize how effective it is (i.e, not very).

Part of being an effective DBE marketer is recognizing when your team — or you, for that matter — are sprinting ahead without checking your destination. Be willing to push "pause" and reassess your goals and activities.

As leaders in DBE, we must resist the temptation to see activity as progress. As you hack your way through the jungle, it's not just the fact that you're "moving forward" that matters:

> **"** *The leader is the one who climbs the tallest tree, surveys the situation, and yells, 'Wrong jungle!' ... Busy, efficient producers and managers often respond ... 'Shut up! We're making progress!'"*
>
> — Steven Covey

Brands get into the wrong jungle with their digital marketing in innumerable ways; and by the time you finish reading this paragraph, someone will have come up with another one! It's worth noting some common missteps that come up in many of our DBE workshops. Consider these slip-ups as you develop your plan for ongoing calibration:

Common ways companies get off track and how to get back on

Tactic du jour: Implementing a new tactic because it's trending or seems exciting to the twenty-something's in the firm, or worse yet, the CEO's nephew.

How it happens: New tactics and tools are constantly becoming available, so quickly in fact, that you can easily pivot every week into a new one. The latest-and-greatest tools are often tempting because new and shiny things are inherently interesting to us. Marketers are good at marketing, so new marketing ideas are often very well promoted and seem to suddenly be everywhere.

Why it's a problem: Unless a new approach aligns with your defined strategy, it's more likely to become a distraction than a means to move your brand forward. The toughest tactic du jour to handle is the one recommended by management. We've often seen non-marketers at the SVP or C-level get excited about a new social media platform, marketing automation tool, or "killer new SEO technique" and insist it be implemented as the top priority. This rarely goes well, of course.

How to fix it: Be prepared for the onslaught of tactics du jour and stay on track in three key ways (two of which relate directly to principles outlined in this book):

- **Work from a plan.** By having a clearly articulated plan, you'll be able to evaluate new ideas against it and determine whether they're beneficial before implementing them.

- **Work toward well-defined goals.** Similarly, clearly defined goals allow you to ask of any new tactic, "How will this improve our performance toward our established goals?"

And the third and most important defense against tactics du jour:

- **The best defense is a good offense.** Consistently hit your marketing goals. Make sure your goals are well-defined, quantitative, and realistic (and this may take some work; you'll need to educate your management team). Next, ensure you deliver on them. If you want to be able to tell management, "Thanks, but we've got this," when they suggest launching a Snapchat campaign for your new financial services product, you'll want to do that from a position of strength.

Going stale: Carrying on with the same plan even when it's not working

This could be called the corollary of the tactic du jour. Whereas with chasing shiny new things tends to change tactics too often (without thinking them through), in this opposite case, stagnation develops. Going stale represents a nasty habit of continuing to do the same thing because "that's how we do it here," even if there's evidence that it no longer works.

How it happens: The two most common causes of this behavior could be summed up as survivorship bias (a.k.a success bias) and observation bias.

Survivorship bias suggests that if you only examine successful companies, you can easily mistake their strategies for successful strategies. Just because Starbucks uses green in its logo doesn't mean a green logo will lead your company to success. We use the term "success bias" to mean a survivorship bias of one's own ideas. That is, when a person or a company has employed a certain tactic and has achieved success, it's often assumed that tactic caused the success, without any real testing. It can be extremely difficult to change the mind of a so-called successful executive about certain approaches that have "always worked," even when there's good evidence demonstrating those approaches no longer get results. Unsophisticated marketers (or non-marketers), may fail to see how the market has evolved, and will typically continue to repeat the same tactics for years as they steadily decline in their effectiveness.

Observation bias is closely related to survivorship bias but comes from having too narrow of a viewpoint about what might be causing a certain situation or trend in the business. If every time sales drop, you change the campaign creative; or if every time your site traffic slows, you get a new SEO person, you may be experiencing observation bias.

A policeman sees a drunk man searching for something under a streetlight and asks what he has lost. He says he lost his keys, and they both look under the streetlight together. After a few minutes the policeman asks if he is sure he lost them here, and the drunk replies, no, he lost them in the park. The policeman asks why he is searching here, and the drunk replies, "The light is better here."

–The "Streetlight Effect", a parable of observational bias

Why it's a problem: A particular strategy should be carried on as long as it produces results — but not longer. While abandoning a historically effective strategy when you have a down month is probably irrational, it's even more irrational to keep the status quo going when a downtrend continues. Market conditions change, demographics shift, and consumer tastes are notoriously fickle. Adapting to these changes is a critical part of any DBE strategy.

How to fix it: It takes real maturity to see your own biases for what they are, be willing to let go of unsuccessful approaches, and step out of the organizational comfort zone in search of new ways to market. Acknowledge these biases. Bring them out into the open.

- Use data rather than anecdotes to support a strategy.

- Ask yourself questions like, "What are we afraid to ask in this company?" or "What options are automatically off the table without discussion?"

- Seek out contrary opinions. Ask a colleague to poke holes in your strategy.

- Commit yourself to the steps you will take based on an experiment, such as an A/B test, before you run the test.

- Notice when you secretly don't want a tactic to work and look carefully at the reasons why.

Management by catastrophe: Adjusting only when things go horribly wrong

It's natural, and generally a good idea, to make changes when a crisis occurs. However, this is not the best time to adjust; and it certainly should not be the only time.

Why it happens: A crisis, such as crashed sales or a missed launch, can trigger a lot of self-examination within a company. But it's easy to forget that a crisis is often just a bunch of separate, smaller problems that weren't addressed, that suddenly built up to critical mass, and exploded all at once. Put off changing the oil in the car long enough, neglect to renew your AAA membership, and forget to charge your mobile phone, and before you know it you're hiking your way across town. The real reasons for the small omissions that led to the crisis can be overshadowed by the crisis itself, leading to bad decisions.

Why it's a problem: First, in business as in life, you won't make your best decisions when you're upset and everyone is mad at everyone else. Anger and stress increase bias, reduce people's ability to observe and analyze data, and tend to cause us to jump into familiar patterns of "solutions" that may not have anything to do with the situation (like firing the marketing director, getting a new agency, throwing out the marketing plan, etc.). Second, and more importantly, the fallacy that you're dealing with a single-point "crisis" (e.g., crashed second-quarter sales) can distract you and your colleagues from looking for and addressing the numerous inputs that led to that unexpected crash in the first place. It's likely they were actually measurable, detectable, and fixable at the time they occurred.

How to fix it: The essence of this one is routine. The monthly progress report, the quarterly deep evaluation of analytics, and the consistent tracking and review of data will protect you. If you're consistently tracking lead data, you should see a sales crash coming weeks or even months beforehand, giving you the time to plan a solution so the crash never occurs. Likewise, underperforming campaigns, strategies, or even personnel can be corrected, trained, and optimized, before the underperformance becomes critical. Applying the information under "Building the habit" in the section above is a sure-fire way to catch problems early and stay on track.

Calibrate your way to greatness: Building a culture of continuous improvement

One of the most powerful aspects of DBE is its inherent measurability. The capacity to continuously monitor, tweak, and adjust in response to a dynamic environment allows for optimization over time.

Just as nature has evolved ever more effectively and streamlined organisms by constantly weeding out unsuccessful strategies and rewarding successful ones, today's (and tomorrow's) business environment tests, rejects, and rewards companies at an unimaginable pace. The same can and should be true within firms: New ideas must constantly be tested and the great ones scaled up quickly, while the not-so-great ideas are quickly discarded.

As marketers in DBE, we have the ability to bring this capacity full circle. In other words, we can build a culture (not only in our marketing departments, but also in our companies) of candid, transparent feedback and continuous improvement. By continually checking and quantifying our performance — calibrating — and examining our goals and expectations — resetting — we can steadily evolve toward greatness.

Wrapping It Up:
DBE and the Future

> ❝ *The only thing that is constant is change"*
> — Heraclitus (535 - c. 475 BCE)

If you've ever felt that you're living in the fastest and most chaotic time in the history of the world, you're not alone. People have been thinking the same thing for at least 3,000 years.

You'd think we'd have gotten used to it by now.

But it's a fact that the pace of change in our environment has been accelerating since the days when the first marketers advertised their hunting skills with clay paint on the wall of a cave.

Just as early tribes who learned to fashion stone tools were able to out-compete their slower-learning brethren for scarce resources, today's marketer must constantly innovate and remain attuned to what's coming next.

The tools of tomorrow will yet again eclipse the ones we have today.

Virtual reality promises to rewire our whole concept of social networking and digital relationships. When another person on the other side of the planet (or a digital avatar that lives only in a server) can seem as real as your spouse in the next room, the very idea of sharing will be redefined.

Artificial intelligence, already a part of our lives via narrowly defined devices (whether Google search, Alexa, or Siri), is accelerating and becoming integrated more and more into the basic fabric of reality. Soon AI will not be something we engage with consciously, but rather a distributed force that surrounds us at all times, directing our consciousness in unpredictable ways for better or worse.

And just as every new technology, from cave paint to digital video, has ultimately become part of the marketer's tool kit, so, too, these and other innovations will come to be a part of yours. How you integrate them, and how you choose the tools and strategies that best suit your objectives, will be the measure of your success as a DBE marketer.

It's the nature of this book to function as a snapshot in time, so eventually many of the anecdotes we've discussed here may have faded into obscurity (and by then I will have moved on to a new edition); but that's exactly why we've devoted this guide to core principles that will hold from next year and through 2050 and beyond:

1. **Know your audience.** Learn to listen before you speak, so you can create something that will truly bring value to those for whom it's created.

2. **Give your audience a reason to engage with your brand.** No one owes you their time and attention, especially today's busy consumer. Make it worth their while.

3. **Stand for something.** Brands and organizations that express an opinion and are willing to make a stand for their beliefs have always stood out from the noise.

4. **Develop discipline.** It's not enough to invent a great brand story. To build trust, you must ensure it's articulated in everything your brand touches.

5. **Work collaboratively across disciplines.** DBE takes a variety of specialists — strategy, creative UI/UX, technology, content development, and more. Make sure each discipline engages in good communication with one another.

6. **Set goals, and measure the right things.** Work toward clearly defined objectives, and seek to make those measures both qualitative and quantitative.

7. **Periodically calibrate and reset.** Every great expedition has required some course correction to reach its objective. Adjusting your plans or tactics should not be feared, but embraced — as long as it keeps your goal in sight and moves you closer to it.

> ❝ *As to methods there may be a million and then some, but principles are few. The man who grasps principles can successfully select his own methods. The man who tries methods, ignoring principles, is sure to have trouble.*❞
>
> — Harrington Emerson, as quoted in "The Typography of Advertisements that Pay," published by Gilbert P. Farrar in 1917

As a bottom line, here's our advice: learn the principles outlined in this book. Use them to create a foundation that supports your marketing efforts even in the most chaotic of business environments. The tougher the elements, the stronger — and more flexible — we must make our shelters in order to withstand them.

Even more important, become a teacher of these ideas. Marketing no longer ends at the door of the marketing department. In the best organizations, it's a part of every activity, from product design to customer service.

By integrating the principles of DBE into every facet of your organization, you'll have the potential to create truly ground-breaking results for your organization.

We look forward to hearing about your accomplishments. Email me at DBE@L7Creative.com

7 Principles of Digital Brand Engagement

As a modern marketer, you need Digital Brand Engagement (DBE) to adapt and thrive in a rapidly evolving market.

1 Know Your Audience — and Yourself

A disciplined process includes primary research and thoughtful evaluation to pin down the decision-making criteria of your audience.

5 Work Collaboratively Across Disciplines

Information, results, analytics, and trends must be coordinated between disciplines to achieve a consistent brand story and effectively optimize your DBE campaigns.

6 Set Goals, and Measure the Right Things

Quality DBE campaigns set both quantitative and qualitative goals.

2 Give Your Audience a Reason to Engage

Authentic engagement with your target customer is an incredibly valuable and scarce commodity.

3 Stand for Something

Don't be afraid to shout that your brand stands for something. Being consistent, transparent, and bold gives your brand purpose.

4 Develop Discipline

Adopt the habits necessary to ensure your foundation is not only maintained, but is building a powerful and lasting digital presence.

7 Periodically Calibrate and Reset

It is critical to periodically review your progress against your goals and make the appropriate course corrections to stay on track.

You can download a copy of this infographic here: l7creative.com/digital-brand-engagement-book

www.ingramcontent.com/pod-product-compliance
Lightning Source LLC
Chambersburg PA
CBHW070941210326
41520CB00021B/7001